Reading's Influe........ ......

Terry Dixon was born in Tilehurst, Reading, and held the post of National Publicity and Development Officer on the National Federation of 18 Plus Groups NEC for 6 years. In his day job he was an electronics engineer and project manager. Taking early retirement in 2016, he started 'Terry's Reading Walkabouts' to get fitter, and to introduce visitors and residents to the hidden culture and history of Reading. In 2017 he decided to celebrate Vote 100 by creating a new guided walk called 'Famous/not-so-famous women of Reading' which was launched in February 2018 to coincide with the date the Act of Parliament received royal assent. His research for that walk is the basis for this book. His walkabouts have raised over £7500 (including £1000 for Berkshire Women's Aid) for local charities and he is a member of Reading Civic Society's committee.

Linda Saul was born and raised on the Isle of Wight but has lived in Reading for about 35 years. After studying at Cambridge, she embarked on a successful career in IT. In her younger, wilder, days she developed a habit of falling out of aircraft before finally learning to fly one. She is now a full-time artist, her work focusing on the built environment. She exhibits regularly in London and is an active member of the Reading Guild of Artists. A perpetual student, she has completed a physics degree with the Open University and is now studying for a Masters in mathematics. In 2019 Linda co-curated an exhibition of art inspired by Oscar Wilde's *The Ballad of Reading Gaol*. Galvanised by the campaign to save Reading Gaol for the town, she conceived and organised the Reading Gaol Hug with the help of many others, including Terry.

Also published by Two Rivers Press

The Whole Story: Painting more than just the flowers
  by Christina Hart-Davies
The Art and History of Whiteknights edited by Jenny Halstead
The Art of Peter Hay by John Froy with Martin Andrews
Signs of the Times: Reading's Memorials by Malcolm Summers
Rural Reading by Adrian Lawson & Geoff Sawers
The Constitutionals: A work of fiction by Peter Robinson
Botanical Artistry: Plants, projects & processes by Julia Trickey
The Greenwood Trees: History, folklore and uses of Britain's trees
  by Christina Hart-Davies
Reading Abbey and the Abbey Quarter by Peter Durrant & John Painter
Reading's Bayeux Tapestry by Reading Museum
*A Coming of Age: Celebrating 18 Years of Botanical Painting by the Eden
  Project Florilegium Society* by Ros Franklin
Picture Palace to Penny Plunge: Reading's Cinemas by David Cliffe
The Shady Side of Town: Reading's Trees by Adrian Lawson & Geoff Sawers
Reading: The Place of the People of the Red One by Duncan Mackay
Silchester: Life on the Dig by Jenny Halstead & Michael Fulford
The Writing on the Wall by Peter Kruschwitz
Caught on Camera: Reading in the 70s by Terry Allsop
Plant Portraits by Post: Post & Go British Flora by Julia Trickey
Allen W. Seaby: Art and Nature by Martin Andrews & Robert Gillmor
Reading Detectives by Kerry Renshaw
Fox Talbot & the Reading Establishment by Martin Andrews
All Change at Reading by Adam Sowan
Cover Birds by Robert Gillmor
Caversham Court Gardens: A Heritage Guide by Friends of Caversham
  Court Gardens
Birds, Blocks & Stamps: Post & Go Birds of Britain by Robert Gillmor
Down by the River: The Thames and Kennet in Reading by Gillian Clark

Reading's Influential Women

Terry Dixon & Linda Saul

TWO
RIVERS
PRESS

First published in the UK in 2020 by Two Rivers Press
7 Denmark Road, Reading RG1 5PA
www.tworiverspress.com

ISBN 978-1-909747-62-3

1 2 3 4 5 6 7 8 9

Two Rivers Press is represented in the UK by Inpress Ltd
and distributed by NBNi.

Cover illustrations by Martina Hildebrandt
Text and cover design by Nadja Guggi and typeset in Parisine

Printed and bound in Great Britain by TJ International, Padstow

Acknowledgements

We would like to thank the many people who have helped us draw this book together in various ways. Jackie Dixon for her unstinting support, adding the odd gem, typing, realism when required, and being my rock (Terry). Adrian Larkham for his support and being a useful sounding board (Linda). Ruth Dalfson for contributing her expertise in the early stages of developing the text, finding and checking facts like dates and places of birth. Rachel Eden for providing the spark that inspired Terry's 'Vote 100 – Women of Reading' Walkabouts and for the foreword. Helen Lambert, Hester Casey, Jessica Swale and Fiona Talkington for providing source material. Martina Hildebrandt, Carole Stephens and Martin Andrews for their generosity and skill in providing inspiring illustrations. Richard Bennett for his knowledge and support. Mark Thompson for taking part in both 'Vote 100 – Women of Reading' Walkabouts and his support. Lizzie Dunford & Jen Harris at the Jane Austen House Museum, Tom Holmes at Reading Football Club, Colin Boyes at Thames Valley Police Museum, Julia Gault at Mitcham Cricket Club, Sophie Howe at ourberylcook.com and Caroline Benson at MERL for their help sourcing photographs and artwork. And all at Two Rivers Press: Sally Mortimore, Barbara Morris, Anne Nolan and Nadja Guggi in particular, for their help in turning Terry's initial concept into this book. Being a dyslexic engineer, co-writing a book was never on his bucket list! Thanks are also due to Jill Swale, Melanie Stiassny, Ann Berne, Christopher Campbell Howes and Dr Tess Millar.

The authors' royalties are to be donated to Berkshire Women's Aid (www.berkshirewomensaid.org.uk) in recognition of their long term work in Reading.

Publisher's acknowledgements

Two Rivers Press would like to acknowledge the support of our community which has enabled us to keep publishing despite the disruption to our business that COVID-19 caused, and to thank Jane Club (UK) for their sponsorship of this publication.

Picture credits

Martina Hildebrandt: p. 4 Empress (Maude) Matilda; p. 10 Jane Austen; p. 12 Mary Russell Mitford; p. 15 Frances Dann, Elizabeth Waterhouse; p. 18 Amelia Dyer; p. 19 Professor Edith Morley; p. 23 Phoebe Cusden; p. 29 Lady Eve Balfour; p. 30 Evelyn Dunbar; p. 41 Alma Cogan; p. 44 Ann Packer; p. 45 Jacqueline Bisset; p. 55 Miranda Krestovnikoff; p. 57 Molly Hide, Claire Taylor; p. 61 A field hockey player; p. 62 Deborah Flood, Anna Watkins; p. 66 Fran Kirby

Linda Saul: p. 5 Hospitium; p. 7 *Reading Mercury* offices; p. 14 Dann's Photographers; p. 34 Spitfire instrument panel and Miles Master aircraft

Martin Andrews: p. 26 Dr Ethelwynn Trewavas; p. 33 Elizabeth Taylor; p. 51 Babita Sharma; p. 60 Kate and Helen Richardson-Walsh; p. 69 Coralie Bickford-Smith

Carole Stephens: p. 27 *Labeotropheus trewavasae*; p. 42 Janet Reger; p. 46 Jacqueline Bisset; p. 48 Marianne Faithfull

Salvo Toscano: p. 9 Tutu Melaku; p. 70 Suzanne Stallard

Museum of English Rural Life (MERL), University of Reading: p. 13 Mary Russell Mitford; p. 28 Lady Eve Balfour

Richard Claypole: p. 67 Fran Kirby; p. 68 Fara Williams

Peter Hay: p. 8 Reading Sauce

Jane Austen's House Museum: p. 11 Jane Austen House & banknote

Thames Valley Police Museum: p. 17 Amelia Dyer

University of Reading, Special Collections: p. 20 Edith Morley

Mark Thompson: p. 24 Düsseldorf Wall

Christopher Campbell Howes: p. 31 Evelyn Dunbar

Richard Bennett: p. 36 Molly Casey

ourberylcook.com: p. 39 Beryl Cook paintings

Marie Pridham: p. 49 Iris Pridham

Anouska Henderson: p. 53 Fiona Talkington

Terry Dixon: p. 59 Kate Winslet 'Classic Titanic pose'

Michael Wharley FBIPP: p. 65 Jessica Swale

Contents

Foreword | 1
Introduction | 2

Reading's Influential Women | 4

Empress (Maude) Matilda | 4
Kate Middleton, Duchess of Cambridge | 6
Elizabeth Anne Le-Noir | 6
Ann Cocks | 8
Tutu Melaku | 9
Jane Austen | 10
Mary Russell Mitford | 12
Frances Dann & Fanny Lewis | 14
Elizabeth Waterhouse | 15
Lady Harriet Wantage | 16
Yasmina Siadatan | 16
Amelia Dyer | 17
Professor Edith Morley | 19
Lilian Augusta Fontaine | 21
Francesca Longrigg | 21
Victoria Summer | 22
Eliza Bennett | 22
Phoebe Cusden | 23
Theresa May | 26
Dr Ethelwynn Trewavas | 26
Lady Evelyn Balfour | 29
Sarah Beeny | 30
Evelyn Dunbar | 30
Kate Humble | 32
Elizabeth Taylor | 32
Lettice Curtis | 34
Maxine 'Blossom' Miles | 35
Molly Casey | 36
Baroness Angela Browning | 37
Beryl Cook | 38
Alma Cogan | 40

Janet Reger | 42
Alana Morshead | 43
Ann Packer | 44
Jaqueline Bisset | 45
Lisa Daniely | 46
Cherith Mellor | 47
Marianne Faithfull | 47
Sally Oldfield | 48
Iris Pridham | 49
Ivy Hewitt | 50
Sally Taylor | 50
Sangeeta Bhabra | 50
Babita Sharma | 51
Laura Tobin | 52
Lucy Benjamin | 52
Fiona Talkington | 53
Lucy Worsley | 54
Miranda Krestovnikoff | 55
Molly Hide | 56
Claire Taylor | 56
Kate Winslet | 58
Anna Winslet | 58
Beth Winslet | 59
Kate Richardson-Walsh | 60
Helen Richardson-Walsh | 61
Alex Danson | 61
Deborah Flood | 62
Anna Watkins | 63
Rebecca Cooke | 63
Natalie Dormer | 64
Jessica Swale | 64
Fran Kirby | 66
Fara Williams | 68
Coralie Bickford-Smith | 69
Suzanne Stallard | 70
Mary Genis | 71
Hannah (Callowhill) Penn | 71

Further reading | 74

Foreword

Reading is a diverse and wonderful town. We could be even better, and one of the best ways to encourage us to strive to improve is to learn more about those who came before us and shaped our town.

Ironically, because of our success, sometimes our rich history is overlooked. Over the last few years, Terry has been doing his utmost to help change that by leading a variety of guided walks around the town's historical sites and at the same time has been raising money for local charities.

He was one of the most enthusiastic supporters of the events to mark Vote 100 in Reading – 100 years since women got the vote. One of the things we discovered during that year was the extent of the contribution that the women of Reading have made to our town. Some of them are famous, others well known, and some you may never have heard of. This collection will go some way to redressing the balance.

Cllr Rachel Eden, Vote 100 Reading Coordinator

Introduction

There are innumerable men and women from Reading, UK, who have achieved significant things or contributed to the life of the town and/or the wider world. Some, unfortunately, have gone unrecognised or are forgotten. Also, we know that in the past, the contribution of women was often dismissed, overlooked or attributed to somebody else. We can't hope to document all those women connected to Reading who deserve to be mentioned but we can raise the profile of some, especially those whose connection to Reading is relatively unknown.

To be included in this book, women need to have been born, bred, educated in the greater Reading area, or to have lived there, or else have made an indelible mark on the town.

There are women of Reading who have achieved great things in the third millennium; these have been included. Here the sin of omission is probably more serious, and may become glaringly obvious, but we had to take a snapshot in time. We expect in the future to be kicking ourselves about some of these.

There are also countless women who do good on the quiet, never really achieving recognition. We have included a couple of 'unsung heroines', but we know there are many more.

Many of the women in this book will have had their lives affected by misogyny. Several have played their part in challenging such attitudes. Edith Morley was a Suffragist (although Lady Wantage was anti-suffragism), Ethelwyn Trewavas campaigned for married women to be able to keep their jobs. Some, such as Lettice Curtis, just got on and proved how good they were in a field dominated by men.

Modern campaigns, such as Me Too, and the under-representation of women in many fields and the top tiers of organisations remind us there is still more progress to be made.

One area which has seen massive improvement in recent years is sport. Elite sportswomen are clearly influential in encouraging wider participation in sport, at all levels, and we have several examples in this book. But who knows how many more there might have been if women's sport had not been discouraged in the not-too-distant past.

Patronising attitudes about femininity, the perceived negative effect of physical exercise on reproduction and straight-forward prejudice, did not completely prevent women's football and cricket from enjoying some popularity historically. There were even professional women cricketers at the end of the 18th century. During and after the First World War women's football was a popular spectator sport, possibly the reason for the Football Association's 1921 announcement that football was 'quite unsuitable for females'[1] and banning it on its affiliated clubs' grounds – a ban that lasted until it could be challenged under the 1975 Sex Discrimination Act. Such institutionalised sexism also made it very difficult to become an official or sit on administration boards. The media has also been blamed for under-reporting of women's sport, so a shout-out is due to the *Reading Mercury* (fore-runner of the *Reading Chronicle*) for possibly the first ever newspaper report on a women's cricket match, in 1745.

Just as we are finalising the text of this book, COVID-19 has begun to bite, turning normal life upside down. Many otherwise ordinary people have become heroines and heroes fighting on the front line – doctors, nurses and emergency services, backed up by volunteers, scientists, teachers and those in essential services such as food retailing and refuse collection to name but a few. We salute them all.

In writing this book some interesting threads emerged, and there are always questions. It is fun to try to find any connections between the individuals – were Jane Austen and Mary Mitford friends? Is it co-incidence that one of the first female professional photographers set up a business in the same town where William Fox Talbot had made major advances in photography just a decade earlier? The importance of Jane Austen becomes very apparent when you realise how many of the lives *in this book* have been influenced by her.

Most of these women are 'inspirational' in some way or another. But Linda insisted we include a token baddie, and we have an undisputed winner of that prize; read on to discover who.

Deciding on a structure for this book has been a challenge and was not easy to finalise. We decided upon including historical figures more or less chronologically by birth. More recent women have been grouped alongside others with whom there are (sometimes tenuous) connections. Hence, we kick off with two royal figures separated by almost a millennium.

Reading's Influential Women

Empress (Maude) Matilda

Matilda, the daughter of one king and mother of another, never quite became Queen of England. She was born in 1102 at Sutton Courtenay, near Reading, to King Henry I and his first wife, Matilda of Scotland. Aged six, Matilda was betrothed to Heinrich V, the Holy Roman Emperor. She travelled to Germany to marry before her twelfth birthday and was crowned Empress of Rome in 1117. They had no children. Following the Emperor's death, she returned to England. She brought with her part of the imperial treasury including the hand of St James, an important relic she presented to Reading Abbey, which her father had founded in 1121.

Her second arranged marriage was to Geoffrey of Anjou, with whom she had three sons. Her younger brother William Adelin had died in the White Ship Disaster (a tragedy that is thought to have influenced Henry to build Reading Abbey). This made Matilda King Henry's only legitimate offspring. He nominated her as his heir, forcing a reluctant court to swear allegiance to her. The resulting succession crisis was to cause a civil war known as 'the Anarchy' that would last for 18 years.

King Henry died suddenly in 1135 and Matilda's cousin Stephen of Blois seized the throne with the support of the Church and a number of barons. Matilda returned to England in 1139 to claim her throne, supported by her half-brother Robert of Gloucester. Stephen was captured during the Battle of Lincoln.

Victorious, Matilda made her way to London, visiting her father's tomb at Reading Abbey *en route*. In Reading she found support from the townspeople. However, on arrival in London, where she intended to be crowned, she was thwarted by angry crowds and a rival Matilda, Stephen's queen, encamped with an army outside the city. Empress Matilda was forced to retreat. Robert was then captured at the Rout of Winchester and was exchanged for Stephen in a prisoner swap.

Opposite page:
Hospitium of St John

That winter the Empress was besieged in Oxford Castle but escaped. The bloodbath continued but in 1148 she returned to Normandy leaving her eldest son Henry to continue the fight. In 1153 a peace settlement was reached in the Treaty of Winchester. Stephen, bereaved of his wife and his heir, agreed to recognise Henry as his successor. Henry succeeded Stephen in 1154.

Matilda spent the rest of her life in Normandy. She died in 1167 and was buried at Fontevrault Abbey. It is thought that some of her entrails were brought to Reading for burial. We probably have Matilda to thank for Reading's Hospitium. The Shrine of St James's Hand drew pilgrims to Reading Abbey and in 1189 the Hospitium of St John was founded to accommodate the increasing numbers. It is one of just two abbey buildings that stand intact today.

Kate Middleton, Duchess of Cambridge

The Duchess of Cambridge, born Catherine Elizabeth Middleton in the Royal Berkshire Hospital, Reading, married Prince William at Westminster Abbey in April 2011. Their three children, Prince George, Princess Charlotte and Prince Louis, are third, fourth and fifth in line to the throne. Their official residence is Kensington Palace. Besides undertaking royal duties in support of The Queen, The Duchess supports several charitable causes and organisations, many in support of children achieving the best possible start in life. Kate's family still live locally.

Elizabeth Anne Le-Noir

Elizabeth was born in London, the daughter of a famous poet, Christopher Smart, in 1754/5. When her father was admitted to an asylum, Elizabeth, sister Marianne and mother Anna Maria moved to Reading. Anna Maria took over the management of the *Reading Mercury* newspaper (one of the first in England), owned by her step-father, John Newbury. Ultimately it was inherited by Elizabeth and Marianne.

In the 1760s Elizabeth and Marianne, being Catholics, spent three years in a convent in Boulogne. In 1789 the Catholic community in Reading assisted refugees from the French Revolution and Elizabeth went on to marry one of them, the Chevalier John Baptiste Le Noir. Elizabeth opened a boarding school with her niece Eleanora Cowslade, whom she had adopted. The school moved to the Caversham Priory in 1830.

Elizabeth had been discouraged from writing by her mother. She once wrote 'I was born under a cloud where discouragement on the part of others and diffidence on my own have always left me'.[2] At the age of 50 she finally started publishing novels and poetry. Her admirers included **Mary Russell Mitford**, who wrote that her 'books when taken up one does not care to put down again'.[2] She died at Caversham Priory in 1841 at the age of 86.

Reading Mercury newspaper offices in Valpy Street, Reading, as they might have looked

Ann Cocks

Ann Cooper, born in 1763, was the youngest of seven children. Her family in Caversham had been down on their luck and regularly receiving parish relief when, in 1794, she married a local fishmonger called James Cocks. At their property in Duke Street, Ann and James devised a fish sauce that they first marketed in 1802 as 'Reading Sauce'. The ingredients included soy, anchovies, mushroom ketchup, walnut ketchup, chillies and garlic.

The sauce was very successful and soon Cocks & Co were selling it all over the country and in Europe. In 1814–1815 two court cases were won, protecting against fake Reading Sauce products. Phileas Fogg, in Jules Verne's *Around the World in Eighty Days*, liked Reading Sauce on his breakfast.

James Cocks died in 1827, leaving 20 per cent of shares of the business to each of his three sons and 40 per cent to Ann. Ann died 5 years later, leaving the sons running the business. In the 1830s they purchased new premises on the King's Road, where Reading Central Library now stands.

In due course there do appear to have been other manufacturers that made a Reading Sauce; there are references in literature, by Lewis Carroll amongst others, to 'Harvey's Reading Sauce'. However, Cocks &

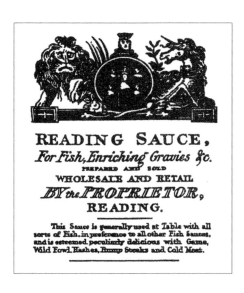

Co laid claim to originating the name. In 1871 the court case of Cocks v Chandler established that although Cocks didn't own a trademark for 'Reading Sauce', only Cocks & Co could call their sauce the *Original* Reading Sauce – for anyone else to do so was misrepresentation.

The company was sold by the Cocks family in 1901. It also made other products, in particular pickles. In the Second World War the company provided piccalillis to the Royal Navy. Unfortunately, they appear to have been usurped in the sauce business by an upstart called Lea & Perrins, established in 1837, who started to outsell them with their new Worcestershire Sauce. Cocks & Co continued to trade until 1962.

Tutu Melaku

Tutu Melaku was born in Addis Ababa, Ethiopia. She came to Reading in 1991 when her then-husband was studying for a PhD at the university.

Having grown up in a large family that regarded food and cooking with enthusiasm, it is unsurprising that, after a period cleaning university halls of residence, she decided to set up her own catering business. This eventually led to *Tutu's Ethiopian Table* opening at the Reading International Solidarity Centre (RISC) where it remained for several

Tutu Melaku © Salvo Toscano

years. She has also introduced *Tutu's Sauces*, a range of Ethiopian sauces that enables people to savour her food at home. In 2019 Tutu moved her cafe to the Palmer Park Lodge. The opening was attended by the Ethiopian Embassy's Deputy Head of Mission who described Tutu as an ambassador for Ethiopia.

Tutu and her business have been nominated for countless awards for food and innovation and won a fair few of them.

After an initial culture shock on her arrival in Reading, Tutu is now fully engaged in the Reading community and sees her customers as her extended family. She offers work to refugees and recovering drug addicts and has established *Tutu's Fund for the Future* which supports education projects in Ethiopia and sponsors education of vulnerable Ethiopian children. Projects include the building of classrooms for two schools in a deprived area.

Tutu has been described as an 'inspiration to young black women and girls'[3] and has been influential in raising the profile of black businesswomen in Reading.

Jane Austen

Jane Austen was born in Steventon Rectory near Basingstoke in 1775. The seventh of eight children, she was very close to her only (older) sister, Cassandra.

In 1783 Jane, aged 7, Cassandra (10) and her cousin Jane Cooper (12), were sent to be tutored by Mrs Ann Cawley in Oxford. Later that year Mrs Cawley moved them to Southampton. However, there was typhus in Southampton, brought ashore by troops returning from war abroad. The girls caught it. Mrs Cawley didn't see fit to notify the families, but Jane Cooper did. Both mothers travelled to Southampton. Jane nearly died. Her aunt caught the fever and died after returning to Bath.

In 1785 the family sent Cassandra to the Abbey House School in Reading. Jane, not wanting to be separated from her sister, was adamant that she'd go with Cassandra. Her parents relented. Her mother has been quoted as saying, 'If Cassandra's head had been going to be cut off, Jane would have hers cut off too'.[4] They were there for 18 months, the cost being too high for their parents to continue paying beyond 1786. The Abbey House School is thought to be the basis for Mrs Goddard's School in Jane's book *Emma*. The remainder of Jane's

Jane Austen £10 banknote outside Jane Austen House Museum

education was at home in Steventon. Here her father taught boys and had amassed a library of 500 books. Her brother James, 10 years her senior, directed much of her reading. From about the age of 11 she started to dedicate her spare time to writing. There was also a family tradition of amateur theatrical performances at Steventon every year.

At the end of 1800 Jane's father retired and it was abruptly announced that the family were moving to Bath. Jane was very upset about this. Her brother James and his family moved into Steventon. From this time to about 1804 was a dry period in terms of new writing for Jane – possibly due to unhappiness at living in Bath. Around 1804 she started to write *The Watsons*, later abandoned. Her father died in 1805, leaving Jane, Cassandra and their mother in difficult circumstances. Eventually they moved to live in a cottage in Chawton, on her brother Edward's estate, and Jane lived the rest of her life there. Over the next few years, *Sense and Sensibility*, *Mansfield Park*, *Pride and Prejudice* and *Emma* were published. In 1816 her health started to fail and she died in 1817 in Winchester. *Northanger Abbey* and *Persuasion* were published posthumously.

Mary Russell Mitford

Mary was born in 1787. Her father George had practised as a surgeon and called himself Dr Mitford, but was not strictly qualified to do so. Her mother Mary came from a wealthy family. George was something of a spendthrift and managed to fritter away most of his wife's inheritance.

Mary was given a lottery ticket for her tenth birthday, and her choice of number, 2224, chosen because the digits added up to her age, hit the jackpot, winning £20,000 – about half a million pounds in today's money. Her father proceeded to spend some of the money on a house in Reading, where they lived before moving to Grazeley.

For four years Mary attended a school in Chelsea. She read widely and started to write poetry in her teens. Her first poetry collection, *Poems*, was published in 1810. She also wrote longer poems, which sold well. Samuel Taylor Coleridge read *Christina* and suggested she tried writing drama.

Eventually George's profligate spending forced the family to move to a labourer's cottage at Three Mile Cross. Mary continued to write to support her family and became a successful playwright. She also

had stories published in *The Lady's Magazine*, which led to dramatic increases in sales of the magazine. These stories were then published in a series of volumes called *Our Village*.

Her father died in 1842 leaving debts of about £1000. Mary's friends rallied around and raised £1500. In 1852 Mary was thrown from her carriage and left partially paralysed. She died in 1855.

Mary greatly admired **Jane Austen**'s writing and was influenced by it. There are interesting connections between Mary and Jane. Mary's mother was a neighbour of the Austens and had described Jane as 'the prettiest, silliest, most affected, husband-hunting butterfly'.[5] Jane was 12 years older than Mary but they shared the same birthday, 16 December. The school that Mary went to in Chelsea was the successor to Jane's Abbey House School.

Sketch of Mary Russell Mitford by Daniel Maclise, as published in
The Maclise Portrait Gallery, 1883

Frances Dann's shop in Broad Street, Reading

Frances Dann & Fanny Lewis

Frances Dann (born 1817) opened a photography studio in Broad Street in 1856. As a woman she couldn't be listed as the business owner, so her husband Francis was. It was only one letter out.

The only other professional photographer known to have been in Reading at that time was using the Daguerreotype method, which did not allow multiple copies of an image and was one of the two approaches to photography then available. Frances was using the alternative method that Henry Fox Talbot is famous for pioneering – also in Reading, only a few years previously. This approach caught on and came to dominate photography before the digital era in the 20th century. So Frances Dann was something of a pioneer; she must have been one of the earliest female professional photographers anywhere, but she *was* the first in Reading.

Towards the end of the 19th century a second studio was opened in Oxford Road. When Frances Dann retired her grand-daughter Fanny Lewis (1866) took over the business and the business name changed to Dann-Lewis.

Portraiture was the bread and butter for photographers in those days. However, the studio also specialised in topographical images of Reading, photographing prisoners at the local police station, and assisting the Royal Berkshire Hospital with X-rays.

Dann-Lewis left us a documentary visual record of what Reading looked like between the 1880s and 1930s, when it bustled with industry. Some of the photographs were taken from the top of the Mill Lane Water Tower that used to stand by the Kennet in central Reading, giving aerial views. The University of Reading holds about 2000 glass plates and the photos are accessible via the Museum of English Rural Life (MERL). While 2000 may not sound a lot by today's standards, photography was far more labour intensive in those days.

Elizabeth Waterhouse

Elizabeth Hodgkin was born in Tottenham in 1834. In 1860 she married architect Alfred Waterhouse, and in 1868 he built them a home in Reading, Foxhill House. He also designed the main façade of part of Reading Town Hall, including the clock tower, in 1875.

Elizabeth was active in the Arts and Crafts movement. She set up a night school, the 'Yattendon Guild', for local men and boys to learn craft skills making items from copper and brass. They made decorative objects such as vases from her designs and they were sold at Liberty in London and in the village shop. She also helped provide employment for local women through her embroidery designs.

Elizabeth was also a watercolourist and a published author. Her book, *The Island of Anarchy*, was re-published by Two Rivers Press in 1997. She has been described as 'an artist who could paint but also hammer copper into shape, a writer and thinker fascinated by science and astronomy who loved wild flowers and birds singing. A businesswoman who could also enjoy childhood games, a lady of the manor at the loving centre of the home and a genuine friend to her tenants and servants'.[6]

Lady Harriet Wantage

Harriet Jones-Lloyd, born 1837, was the daughter of a Welsh banker. As his sole heir she was to become one of the wealthiest heiresses of her time. On a tour of Italy at the age of 14 she met her future husband, Robert James Lindsay.

She was an art connoisseur and a great supporter of the National Art Collections Fund. Lady Wantage and her husband helped form the National Aid Society, later to become the British Red Cross Society. In 1883 she was one of the first recipients of the Order of the Red Cross inaugurated by Queen Victoria.

A noted philanthropist, she gave to hospitals and nursing institutions. She was a prominent anti-suffragist, active as the president of the North Berks Anti-Suffrage League. In addition to her fortune she appears to have inherited her views on women's roles from her father, who was strongly against awarding degrees to women, resigning from London University's Senate over it.

In 1908 she gave a hall of residence (for men), Wantage Hall, to the Reading University College. Only Oxford and Cambridge are believed to have had purpose-built halls of residence before Wantage Hall was built. 1908 was the year **Edith Morley** became a professor. We assume they weren't friends.

Lady Wantage died in 1920.

Yasmina Siadatan

Yasmina is half-Iranian and was born in Hull. She grew up in Reading, attending the Kendrick School and going on to read Economic History and Population Studies at the London School of Economics. After working in pubs and restaurants she opened her own restaurant, Mya Lacarte, in Caversham with her brother. In 2009 she appeared on the BBC TV programme *The Apprentice*, which she won and so started work with Sir Alan (now Lord) Sugar.

After a break in which she had two children, she was head-hunted by James Caan, of TV's *Dragon's Den* fame. He was setting up a start-up loans initiative for business backed by the coalition government. Yasmina became the Head of Operations. She has since taken a post as Head of Marketing for a financial services organisation.

Amelia Dyer

Unfortunately, not all of Reading's influential women are memorable in a good way. The 'Reading baby farmer', aka Amelia Dyer (born 1838), is remarkable only in terms of pure evil.

One morning in March 1896 a bargeman recovered a package from the river Thames at Reading and was horrified to find in it the body of a baby girl.

In the subsequent police investigation Detective Constable James Anderson found traces of the address of a Mrs Thomas in Caversham in the paper in which the body had been wrapped. They found her now living in Reading. A young woman arranged a meeting with Mrs Thomas; the young woman was a decoy and it was the police who turned up to discuss her services. Letters and baby clothes found in a

Amelia Dyer

search of her home suggested she was caring for several children, but there were none in the house.

A subsequent search of the river found six more tiny bodies. A baby girl and boy, together in an old carpet bag, were identified, enabling the police to build a case against Mrs Thomas, aka Amelia Dyer.

In Victorian times, it being ruinous to be an unmarried mother, it was not uncommon for single mothers to pay a one-off sum to have their baby brought up by somebody else, often in response to a newspaper advert. With ineffective regulation, this practice was wide open to abuse.

Amelia Dyer would place adverts in newspapers offering to adopt a child into a 'good country home', with prices starting at £10. She started in Bristol, where babies in her 'care' tended to die of neglect. Eventually she refined the process, eliminating the need for a death certificate by disposing of the bodies. This had the benefit of removing the need to wait for the babies to die of starvation, strangling them with tape being much more efficient. In order to stay ahead of the law and parents enquiring about their adopted offspring, she moved frequently, mainly around the Bristol area, before moving to Reading.

It has been estimated that Amelia Dyer may have killed as many as 400 victims, which would make her one of the most prolific serial killers in British and world history. Most of her evil was perpetrated elsewhere – she only lived in Reading briefly – but the Reading Borough Police get the credit for putting an end to her activities. The *Reading Standard* at the time said that the London police had an additional seven cases fully prepared in case the trial based on the Reading cases failed to secure a conviction. She was remanded at Reading Gaol before being tried at the Old Bailey, convicted of the murders of two babies, and hanged at Newgate Gaol on 10 June 1886.

Following this case, laws around adoption and fostering were tightened considerably.

Professor Edith Morley

Edith was born in London in 1875. Her father was a surgeon-dentist. She was the fourth of six children; the only girl. She hated the restrictions on her freedom that being a girl entailed, such as having to wear gloves and a thick veil that was supposed to protect her complexion as a small child, and not being able to play team games. Fortunately, her parents were keen that she received as good an education as her brothers. After college in Kensington she went to a finishing school in Hanover, where she became fluent in French and German.

She studied English at the women's department of King's College, London University. There she played hockey, regarding the club as the most important of the student societies she joined. She passed the Oxford exams, but because she was not a man, she was not awarded a degree. Twenty-seven years later she was awarded an honorary MA by Oxford University.

Edith taught for a while at King's College before becoming an assistant lecturer in English at University College, Reading (later the University of Reading). In 1907, as the college prepared for university status, all the heads of departments were awarded professorships except Edith, the only woman head. She threatened to resign and was awarded a professorship somewhat grudgingly in 1908, making her the first female professor at an English university. She was refused an assistant on the basis that no man would want to work for a woman.

Not surprisingly, Edith was a Suffragist. A protest against taxation without representation resulted in some of her possessions being seized and auctioned off to pay her rates. According to her memoir *Before and After*, most of the college students attended the sale.

In 1908 she became a socialist and joined the Fabian Society, breaking a family tradition of conservatism. During the First World War she worked for the National Council of Women's Voluntary Patrols – a predecessor to women police – and helped Belgian refugees. In 1934 she became a magistrate, and she was a member of the Howard League for Penal Reform. She set up the Reading Refugee Committee in 1938 and campaigned against the conditions in internment camps. She was appointed OBE for her work with refugees in the Second World War.

One of her most famous publications was *Women Workers in Seven Professions*, which she edited. This describes issues encountered by

women in various professions including teaching, medicine and the civil service. Frequent reference is made to the marriage bar – in many professions, including teaching, women were usually forced to retire on marriage, an issue that **Ethelwynn Trewavas** campaigned against.

The University of Reading holds an annual lecture in Edith's honour and the Humanities and Social Sciences building on the Whiteknights Campus was renamed the Edith Morley building in 2017.

Edith died in Reading in 1964.

Lilian Augusta Fontaine

Born in Reading in 1886, Lilian won a music scholarship to Reading College and then attended RADA. She featured in seven Hollywood films in the 1940s and 1950s. These included *Ivy* (1947) and *The Bigamist* (1947), in which her daughter Joan starred. Both her daughters, Joan Fontaine and Olivia de Havilland, won Oscars during their acting careers. She was also a TV actress and coached drama students in a theatre, later renamed The Lilian Fontaine Garden Theatre in Saratoga, California. Lilian died in Santa Barbara, California, aged 88.

Francesca Longrigg

Reading born composer, lyricist, songwriter, author and actor, Francesca Longrigg is known for appearing in *Star Wars: Episode VII – The Force Awakens* (2015), *The Boat That Rocked* (2009) and *Empire of the Sun* (1987). She lived in New York for a while, and there collaborated with reggae artist Floyd Lloyd, co-wrote *It Ain't Easy* with Pink Floyd's Jon Carin and was lead singer with The Prescients. She released the albums *Dark* (2006) and *True Noise* (2017) and provided the voices for two characters in *The Longest Journey*, an award-winning computer game. Francesca married and moved back to London. Daughter Lara (and her messy bedroom) inspired her critically acclaimed children's album *The Land of Sometimes* to become an animated feature film voiced by famous actors.

Victoria Summer

A Reading-born actress and singer, Victoria has been performing since the age of three. She won a scholarship to the Arts Educational School in London. She then worked in musical theatre for several years. Victoria has never been afraid of hard work, taking jobs such as in a hair salon or gym to pay for dancing and singing lessons.

With two suitcases containing all her belongings, Victoria decided to try her luck in film and television in Los Angeles, moving in 2012 to start auditioning. She landed a role in the musical *How Sweet It Is* and released her debut single, *Love Will Have to Wait* (2011).

Her breakthrough was portraying Julie Andrews in the 2013 film *Saving Mr. Banks*, about the making of the Mary Poppins film, and other films followed. She loves animals and is involved in the protection of animal rights, and acts as a spokesperson for veganism.

Eliza Bennett

Eliza is a Reading-born actress, singer and pianist, named after Elizabeth Bennet from **Jane Austen**'s *Pride and Prejudice*. She attended Leighton Park School. Aged 9, Eliza made her professional debut as Jemima in a West End production of *Chitty Chitty Bang Bang*. She played Princess Arabella in her first film *The Prince and Me* (2004) and Tora Abigail Brown in the successful British comedy/fantasy film *Nanny McPhee*. At the age of 14 she starred in *Inkheart* and sang the closing 'My Declaration' recorded at Abbey Road. Eliza trained in dance with Italia Conti and has appeared in West End musicals. She starred as Holly in *Loserville* (2012), for which she earned a Broadway Music World Awards UK for Best Leading Actress nomination. Eliza played Agatha in *The Von Trapp Family: The Life of Music* (2015). British TV appearances include *Broadchurch* (2015) and *Grantchester* (2016), and she appears in US black comedy/drama *Sweet/Vicious* as lead character Jules Thomas.

Phoebe Cusden

Phoebe was born in Reading in 1887. Her father was a farrier and publican and her mother a schoolteacher before she married. Phoebe worked at the telegraphy department at Reading Post Office whilst studying for her City & Guilds at the University Extension College in Reading Hospitium. Becoming Assistant Supervisor with 90 girls and women reporting to her, as a woman she could rise no further.

Phoebe attended **Edith Morley**'s classes at the Workers' Educational Association. They became lifelong friends. Phoebe was also significantly influenced by another socialist, John Rabson, who persuaded her to become a socialist and a union activist. Being a pacifist caused her to leave the Anglican church during the First World War (much later she became a Quaker). This must all have come as a bit of a shock to her Conservative family, especially her devout Anglican mother. Phoebe said, 'When I became a socialist my mother thought that I was going straight to the Devil.'[7]

Above: Cartwheeling Boys, Old Civic Centre, by Brian Slack.
The inscriptions on the plaques read: 'This group of figures of cartwheeling boys was erected to mark the thirtieth anniversary of the
link between Reading and Düsseldorf established by the late Phoebe
Cusden in 1947 when she was mayor of Reading. When, in 1678,
Düsseldorf's Prince Jan Wellem was returning from his wedding, a wheel
of his coach worked loose, a lad sprang forward and turning cartwheels
beside it, held it firm. For this he received a gold ducat. It is still the
tradition for Düsseldorf children to earn a pfennig by turning cartwheels
in the city's main street, the Königsallee.'

A political career followed. She edited the *Reading Citizen*, a Labour newspaper, for many years. Known as 'The Red Woman', she was active during the general strike of 1926 and formed the Reading Women's Labour Party. She stood as a parliamentary candidate for the unwinnable seat of South Berks and in 1931 she was elected to the Council. She fought relentlessly for the disadvantaged – for poor children, better housing and improved conditions in children's homes amongst other causes.

In 1947, when she was mayor, General Collins of the Royal Berkshire Regiment told her of the appalling suffering of people in Düsseldorf, where his regiment was based. In response Phoebe put out an appeal, stating that 'these unfortunate children cannot be held responsible in any way for the guilt of the Nazi Party'.[8] The appeal was a success and food, clothes and toys were collected. She visited the city to see conditions for herself. Housing conditions were intolerable, 40 per cent of the buildings had been destroyed, and food was scarce. At this time other British towns had twinned with towns in other countries, but none with German towns, 'the enemy'. Nevertheless, Phoebe decided to 'adopt' Düsseldorf. She countered objections: 'It would surely be disastrous to any hope of rebuilding Europe on right lines if we allowed the German people to believe (as they are beginning to believe) that we are deliberately starving them.'[9]

Phoebe left the council in 1949. She remained active in the Women's International League for Peace and Freedom and the Campaign for Nuclear Disarmament. In 1970 she finally stood down from the chair of the Reading–Düsseldorf Association, which she had created in 1948. She was showered with honours – an MBE, an honorary doctorate from the University of Reading, *Cusden Way* named after her and, on her final trip to Düsseldorf, the highest honour that city could bestow, the *Verdienstplakette*. She has a blue plaque at 55 Castle Street in Reading, where she once lived, and the Phoebe Cusden Supported Living Scheme (2017) provides 11 eleven much-needed flats with associated support for residents.

She died aged 93. The Düsseldorf Bürgermeister was amongst the dignitaries at her funeral.

Theresa May

Theresa lives just outside Reading between Sonning and Woodley. She was the UK's second female Prime minister, between 2016 and 2019. Previously she had been Home Secretary. She was first elected MP for Maidenhead in 1997, a constituency she still holds. It includes many areas, such as Twyford, that are on the outskirts of Reading.

Dr Ethelwynn Trewavas

Born in Penzance in 1900, Ethelwynn was the eldest of four children. After schooling in Cornwall, she attended Reading University College (now University of Reading), where she graduated in 1921 with an honours degree in zoology and a teaching certificate. She worked for four years as a teacher, coming to the realisation that she would be better as a researcher.

In 1925 she was awarded a scholarship for research by the Household and Social Science Department at King's College for Women in London. She is recorded as pointing out that the research, on the larynx of the frog, made no impact on household or social life. However, this research project contributed to her successful submission for a Doctor of Science degree from the University of London in 1934.

One of her supervisors, Charles Regan, was director of the British Museum (Natural History) and a leading ichthyologist (fish scientist).

Labeotropheus trewavasae named after Ethelwynn

He took Ethelwynn on as a research assistant. She worked at the museum in various capacities until her retirement, continuing her research there until her death. She conducted numerous field studies in Africa, even after retirement. On one such trip she took the opportunity to learn to snorkel, at the age of 80.

During the Second World War she helped evacuate the museum's collections from London. As a member of the Council of Women Civil Servants she campaigned for the lifting of the marriage bar that prevented women in the civil service and government from continuing to work after marriage.

Ethelwynn had a strong interest in cichlid fishes, becoming the world authority on tilapiine cichlids. The high regard she was held in is evidenced by the number of fish with 'trewavasae' or 'ethelwynnae' in their names – she has at least 20 fish species named after her. She was affectionately known as 'E.T.' by colleagues, which is why there is now a genus of fish called 'Etia'. She herself described numerous fish taxa.

During her long and distinguished career she published over 120 papers and books, including a book on cichlid fishes published in 1989, when she was in her late eighties.

Ethelwynn received numerous honours and awards, and died at her home in Reading in 1993.

Lady Eve Balfour

Lady Evelyn Balfour

Lady Eve, born 1898, was the daughter of an earl and niece of a prime minister. She went to Reading University College (now University of Reading) to study a diploma in agriculture in 1915. In 1918 she claimed she was 25 in order to get her first job – running a small farm in Monmouthshire for the Women's War Agricultural Committee. The following year she and her sister, Mary Edith Balfour, purchased a farm in Suffolk.

Apart from farming, she attained a pilot's licence in 1931, played the saxophone, sailed, and wrote detective novels with Beryl Hearnden under the pseudonym Hearnden Balfour.

In the 1930s she became disenchanted with the farming methods of the day. As a tenant farmer on a farm in Haughley, she, with the farm's owner Alice Debenham, initiated an experiment with organic farming.

Her book *The Living Soil* was published in 1943 and reprinted nine times. She was co-founder and first president of the Soil Association from 1946. Her hopes for support from the government for organic methods were thwarted when in 1947 the Agriculture Act committed the country to intensive farming methods following post-war shortages. Lady Balfour retired from the soil association at the age of 85. She died after a stroke, in 1990. The very next day the first grant for farmers wanting to convert to organic farming methods was announced by the Thatcher government.

There is a variety of potato called *Lady Balfour*.

Sarah Beeny

Sarah Beeny is an entrepreneur, property developer and television presenter born in Reading. She grew up south of Reading, in a family with several acres of land and a self-sufficient lifestyle, a large vegetable garden and goats, ducks and chickens. She went to Luckley-Oakfield School in Wokingham and did a foundation course in drama in Basingstoke.

She went into property development with her brother and her husband and landed her first job in television – presenting Channel 4's *Property Ladder* – after a chance meeting at a party with the sister of a television researcher.

Since then she has presented a number of programmes including *Restoration Nightmare* and *Britain's Best Homes* and has written several books, as well as articles for newspapers and magazines.

She has also launched an online estate agent and a dating site.

Evelyn Dunbar

Born in Oxford Street, Caversham, in 1906, Evelyn was the youngest of five children. Her father was a master tailor, her mother a keen gardener, amateur artist and a Christian Scientist. Evelyn went to school in Rochester, then attended the Rochester School of Art before winning a scholarship to study at the Royal College of Art. She first made a name for herself working on a mural commission for a school. She became a freelance painter and illustrator with an interest in gardening and farming.

During the Second World War Evelyn became the only salaried female war artist and was commissioned to record the activities on the Home Front – particularly the Women's Land Army. Paintings would depict farming activities such as pruning, sprout picking, potato sorting and milking practice with artificial udders. She married an RAF pilot who later became an agricultural economist at Oxford.

A Christian Scientist throughout her life, Evelyn's post-war paintings frequently had religious themes. In this respect she has

Opposite page:
Evelyn Dunbar (1906–1960): Self Portrait, 1958. Reproduced by kind permission of Christopher Campbell-Howes.

been compared to the contemporaneous Berkshire artist Stanley Spencer. After 1950 she taught at the Ruskin School of Drawing for many years.

The Tate and the Imperial War Museum have her war paintings in their collections. There has been renewed interest in her work since one of her paintings appeared on television on the *Antiques Roadshow* and was valued at £40,000 – £60,000. A family member, seeing the programme, was prompted to rummage in their attic and 500 previously unknown works were discovered. An exhibition of lost works was held in Chichester in 2016.

Evelyn died in 1960.

Kate Humble

Kate attended the Abbey School in Reading and grew up next to a farm. After school she took a number of odd jobs to fund a year of travel in Africa. Starting as a runner in television, she eventually became a researcher for programmes such as *Animal Hospital* and *The Holiday Programme*. She has also acted. She is now a well-known television presenter on programmes such as *Springwatch*, *Autumnwatch* and *Countryfile*. In *Extreme Wives* she visited communities in Kenya, Israel and India to investigate the roles of women and issues such as female genital mutilation (FGM).

In 2011 she set up a rural skills school on a farm in the Wye Valley.

Kate is passionate about the natural world and naturism and likes to combine the two: 'There's something joyous about it and I urge everyone to try it'.[10]

Elizabeth Taylor

Elizabeth Coles was born in Reading in 1912. Her father was an insurance inspector. She attended the Abbey School and subsequently had jobs as a governess, a tutor and in a library. In her early twenties she joined the communist party, but later transferred her allegiance to Labour. In 1936 she married John Taylor, a chocolate manufacturer.

Elizabeth's first novel, *At Mrs Lippincote's*, was published in 1945. Unfortunately for her, the 1944 film *National Velvet* had started propelling another Elizabeth Taylor towards superstardom. This might be one reason for the author being, as Antonia Fraser described her, 'one of the most underrated writers of the 20th century'.[11] In 1957 Kingsley Amis asked in *The Spectator* 'why it is that so gifted a writer has yet to find the recognition she deserves'.[12]

In total she wrote a dozen novels, four collections of short stories and *Mossy Trotter*, a children's book. Her novel *Angel,* about an author who enjoys success despite her writing being excruciatingly bad, takes place in a fictional town called Norley, which is widely acknowledged to be based on Reading.

Elizabeth was, and still is, a highly regarded writer. Kingsley Amis is quoted as saying she was 'one of the best English novelists born in [the 20th] century',[13] although it is said that it was not novels but short stories that were her forte. Her work tended to focus on daily domestic life, particularly middle-class and upper middle-class and servants' lives. In her introduction to the recent Virago edition of *Angel*, Hilary Mantel described her as 'somewhat underrated' and 'quietly and devastatingly amusing'.[14]

Mrs Palfrey at the Claremont includes a character called Mrs Burton, thought to be a reference to the actress Elizabeth Taylor, who married Richard Burton twice. The book is regarded by many as the author's best novel and was shortlisted for the Booker prize in 1971. It was made into a film in 2005, as was *Angel* in 2007.

Elizabeth Taylor died at the age of 63.

Lettice Curtis

Born in 1915 and raised in Devon, Lettice went on to study mathematics at Oxford University. After graduating she didn't fancy the typical career paths recommended to her – teaching or accountancy. Instead she put a bequest of £100 from her grandmother to good use and learned to fly. Having gained a commercial pilot's licence, she took a job doing aerial surveys. In 1940 she became one of the first women to join the Air Transport Auxiliary (ATA) and started to ferry aircraft about the country to support the war effort. The ATA pilots were a mix of women, pilots from neutral countries and men unable to fly in combat because of age or handicap, which led to the nickname 'Ancient and Tattered Airmen'.

During her time in the ATA Lettice was based at various stations including Hatfield, Hamble and White Waltham near Reading. She flew just about every aircraft type that Britain used in the war, including Spitfires, Hurricanes, Miles Masters, Mosquitos, Wellingtons, Halifaxes and Lancaster bombers. She was the first ATA woman pilot to fly four-engine bombers. In an early victory for gender equality, from 1943 the female ATA pilots were paid the same as the men.

Spitfire instrument panel and Miles Master aircraft

In her autobiography Lettice describes an incident at White Waltham. The Ministry of Aircraft Production had decided that the airfield, which has grass runways, was unserviceable, so the grass was reseeded. When dry weather came, many of the aircraft got punctures. It was discovered that, iron being an important nutrient for grass, a lot of old cutlery had been added to the fertiliser with the grass seed. Knives and forks were embedded in the hard, dry ground. The airfield had to be closed for a while.

After the war Lettice applied for a job as a test pilot at Boscombe Down. Having passed the interview and the flight test, Boscombe wanted to offer her the job. However, gender discrimination reared its ugly head – appointing a woman was a step too far for the Ministry of Supply. She settled for a job as a flight test observer. Later she moved to a similar job at Fairey Aviation back at White Waltham.

Flying was much more than just a job for Lettice. After the war she resumed air racing, often flying a Spitfire. On retirement she rose to the challenge of competitive stamp collecting and was a member of Wokingham Philatelic Society. Needless to say, she kept up her flying and at the age of 77 she acquired a helicopter licence. She also wrote her autobiography and *The Forgotten Pilots*, a history of the ATA. Lettice lived in Twyford for decades and died at the age of 99 in 2014.

Maxine 'Blossom' Miles

Blossom (born 1901), an aviatrix, aircraft engineer, socialite and businesswoman, was married to Frederick George Miles. They designed the Hawk aircraft that was built by Phillips and Powis at Woodley Airfield. They then joined the company that eventually became Miles Aircraft Ltd. The company designed and manufactured numerous aircraft types, including the important Miles Master, which was used as a trainer for Spitfires and Hurricanes in the Second World War. Working alongside her husband on aircraft design, Blossom carried out stress analysis of the designs. She also started the Miles Aeronautical School at Woodley, which taught young people to become aircraft technicians. The school closed in 1948 when the company folded. Blossom was one of five commissioners of the Civil Air Guard, formed in 1938, to recruit a pool of civilian pilots who would be available to help the Royal Air Force in the event of war. Undoubtedly **Lettice Curtis** and Blossom would have met.

Molly Casey

Molly played a large part in saving Reading's historic Town Hall. The Town Hall was designed by Alfred, husband of **Elizabeth Waterhouse** (he also designed London's Natural History Museum, amongst other buildings). Few would deny that it is a stunning building that would be the pride of many a town. And hidden behind it is the beautiful and historic Reading Abbey Hospitium.

However, in the 1970s, Reading Council wanted to bulldoze the Town Hall in order to make way for the Inner Distribution Road (IDR) and a roundabout. Reading Civic Society could see this was a very bad idea. Fortunately, Molly had recently joined the committee. A campaign to save the Town Hall resulted in a last-minute reprieve, and it gained an emergency listed building status.

Molly, born in 1918, went to Kendrick School. She became an inspiring teacher, teaching at E. P. Collier Junior and then Hemdean House School, where she taught English and history for 17 years. She was a pacifist and became a member of the Women's International League for Peace and Freedom, and was involved in the Campaign for Nuclear Disarmament (CND) and the Greenham Common peace camp. It is perhaps not surprising, therefore, that she was a friend of **Phoebe Cusden**.

In addition to her part in saving the Town Hall and the Grade II listed Prospect Park Mansion House (derelict for over 20 years), 'The Molly', as she was sometimes known, successfully proposed that the Concert Hall should be restored as Reading's Millennium Project. Lottery Grant money was obtained and Reading now has an excellent venue, which was formally opened by Prince Edward in 2004.

Molly was a founding member of the Caversham and District Residents' Association (CADRA) and was well known for her campaign to try to save Bugs Bottom in Caversham from development. Using the *Watchdog* byline, she wrote for the *Caversham Bridge* newspaper. She was something of an expert in local history, particularly the civil war, and wrote a history of Hemdean House School.

A replica of a 17th-century wind vane for the refurbished gazebo in Caversham Court Gardens was made and fitted in memory of Molly, who died in 2006.

Baroness Angela Browning

Angela Browning was born in Reading. Her mother worked for the BBC Monitoring service in Caversham; her father at the University of Reading. She attended Westwood Grammar School for Girls in Reading, leaving at 16 to attend Reading Technical College to study home economics and then teacher training at Bournemouth Technical College. Angela then worked in adult education and as an auxiliary nurse in an operating theatre, before setting up her own training consultancy.

Angela first entered parliament as MP for Tiverton, in 1992, serving as an MP for 18 years. During that time she held a number of positions, including Minister of State (Home Office), Shadow Leader of the House of Commons and Shadow Secretary of State for Trade and Industry. Angela was agriculture minister under Prime Minister John Major during the BSE crisis. She was made a life peer in 2010.

She has a son with Asperger's syndrome, and as a back bencher and in the House of Lords Angela has championed support for autism, learning difficulties and mental health issues. A bill she raised under the ten-minute rule was the first step towards getting the Autism Act (2009) on the statute books.

Beryl Cook

Beryl, born in Ogham, Surrey in 1926, was the third of four girls born to mechanical engineer Adrian and office worker Ella. When she was four, Beryl's parents split up and her mother moved to Reading with her daughters. Here Beryl attended Kendrick School and excelled at nothing, not even art. She left school at 14 to train as a typist.

In 1944 the family moved to London. Beryl took various jobs, including chorus girl and model. In 1948 she married her childhood sweetheart, literally the 'boy next door' from Reading, John Cook, by this time a merchant navy officer.

The couple lived for a while in what was then southern Rhodesia and it was there that they gave their ten-year-old son a painting set. Seeing her son's efforts at painting – with a sky at the top, grass at the bottom and nothing in-between – Beryl had a go herself to paint a picture with 'something in the middle'[15] and, to her own surprise, painted a lady with large breasts. Her husband called the painting *The Hangover* and thereafter the painting always hung in their home. However, this wasn't, yet, the start of anything big.

It was about five years later, when the family had moved to Cornwall, that Beryl really started to paint. Her joyful, sometimes saucy, paintings were based on everyday life and typically featured chubby ladies. It has been said that she added weight to her subjects so she didn't have to spend as much time painting the background, which she found boring. The pictures were hung in the family's bed-and-breakfast establishment.

In 1975 the director of the Plymouth Art Centre visited the house, having heard about the paintings, and offered Beryl an exhibition. This was a sell-out and her career took off. Exhibitions in London followed and the following year one of her paintings featured on the cover of *The Sunday Times Magazine*.

In the 1980s she was Britain's most popular living artist. In total, 11 books of her art were published. Her art has been compared with that of Stanley Spencer. She claimed to have been influenced by television cartoons *The Flintstones* and *Yogi Bear.* Her work was, however, perhaps too cheerful and popular to be accepted by the critics or curators of public art collections.

In 1996 she was appointed OBE. She died in 2008.

Hen Party (*top*) and Carnival in Plymouth (*bottom*) by Beryl Cook

Alma Cogan

Born in London into a Jewish family in 1932, Alma was named after silent screen star Alma Taylor. Her father, a costumier, was born in Russia and his family emigrated to England. Her mother, Fanny, a pianist, had played in cinemas accompanying silent films from the age of ten. The family moved to Reading where Alma was educated at St Joseph's Convent School. Aged ten, she made her public debut at a charity concert in Reading at the Palace Theatre. The family then moved to Worthing for a time and Alma studied dress design and sang with a local dance band.

She won a talent contest in Sussex and was auditioned by band leader Ted Heath, who told her to 'come back in six years'.[16] He might have come to regret that; six years later she was a star. A year later she made her first professional stage appearance in Brighton. She then appeared in a London musical, in cabaret and as a film extra. She got a recording contract with HMV and her first record was released in 1952. Dubbed 'the girl with a giggle in her voice' she would sometimes laugh and sing simultaneously.

In the 1950s Alma was frequently on the *BBC Light Programme* radio station (the forerunner of Radio 2) and on television variety shows. A regular on the Morecambe and Wise series *Running Wild*, her first hit song, 'Bell Bottom Blues', sold more than 100,000 copies.

A trademark of Alma's performances was the flamboyant gowns she wore, often designed by herself. They typically had stiff wide skirts that stood up by themselves when she was not wearing them.

She sang some novelty songs, with titles such as 'Never Do A Tango With An Eskimo'. Very popular in the 1950s, she had more hits than any other female singer at the time. She had a No.1 Hit with 'Dreamboat' in 1955 and, the first female British singer to have her own television series, she was for a time the most highly paid female British entertainer.

Alma was very popular in Europe, topping the charts regularly in Sweden and Germany, as well as in Australia and Israel. 'He Couldn't Resist Her with her Pocket Transistor' won her a gold disc and was No.1 in Japan for over a year.

However, with the rise of Rock and Roll her music became unfashionable and her popularity declined in Britain in the 1960s. John Lennon is said to have hated her music and mimicked her when he was a student. Ironically, they were to become very close friends, and were even rumoured to have had an affair.

Alma shared a flat in Kensington with her mother and her sister, the actress Sandra Caron. This was the venue for many parties, and regular visitors included the likes of The Beatles, Princess Margaret, Roger Moore and Noel Coward. Paul McCartney wrote 'Yesterday' at her piano and played the tambourine on the B side of one of her singles.

In 1965 she was admitted to hospital with suspected appendicitis which turned out to be cancer. An operation and brief remission allowed her to do a final tour of Sweden, but she died the following year at the age of 34.

Janet Reger

Janet Phillips was born in London to Jewish immigrant parents in 1935. Her father was a textile manufacturer. The family moved to Reading when the bombing of London during the Second World War started. She attended Kendrick Girls' School, where she excelled at art.

The family's textile business was in decline in the late 1940s, but they had a successful side-line making bras from factory offcuts. Seeing a future in underwear, Janet's father persuaded her to study underwear design at Leicester. She got a lot of publicity for her fashion show at the end of her two-year diploma.

Janet left college in 1953 and had various jobs with underwear and swimwear manufacturers. However, the world was apparently not ready for her adventurous design ideas, so she went to work on a kibbutz in Israel. Here she met Peter Reger, a German whom she married at Reading synagogue in 1961. They lived in Zurich, where she worked as a freelance lingerie designer. In the mid-1960s they moved to London and set up Janet Reger Creations Ltd in 1967, opening their first shop in Knightsbridge, manufacturing glamorous lingerie for the now ready market.

Business boomed. Clientele included royalty and celebrities including Britt Ekland, Princess Diana and Bianca Jagger. They extended production facilities and set up a mail order catalogue as well as supplying boutiques and department stores, and entered the American market in 1976.

In the late 1970s the exchange rate was damaging the export trade to America and the company faced heightened competition. Both marriage and company hit the rocks. In 1983 liquidation of the company resulted in the Janet Reger trademark being sold to Berlei, a company with whom they had previously had a contract. It also led to Peter Reger's suicide.

A fighter as well as an entrepreneur, Janet created a new company, Designs by Janet Reger, which flourished. When, in 1986, Berlei went into receivership she was able to buy back her trademark, at great expense. She made various deals with companies manufacturing bed-linen, soft furnishings and accessories such as glasses to use the Janet Reger brand and it became a household name. This was illustrated by playwright Tom Stoppard, who gave a character the line 'Don't get your Janet Regers in a twist.'[17]

Janet Reger died in 2005.

Alana Morshead

Alana is a Reading-born costume designer and actress now living in Los Angeles. Since attending film school she has been involved in diverse costume design projects including the futuristic film *Equals* (2015), sci-fi drama *One & Two* (2016), *Newness* (2018) and *After* (2019). She has acting credits for several TV shows and produced and directed *Peach Plum Pear* and *The Story of Elle*. Alana has also worked on US TV commercials for the likes of Facebook, Google and Samsung.

Ann Packer

Ann, born in Moulsford, was a member of Reading Athletic Club. Originally a high jumper, she switched to running, winning the English Schools 100 yards in 1959. She also had early success in hurdles and long jump. Ann became a PE teacher, these being the days when even Olympics sportspeople were usually amateurs.

In 1962 she won bronze in the 4×100m relay at the European Championships, and silver in the 4×110 yard relay at the Commonwealth Games. In 1963 she switched events to 400m.

In 1964 she competed in the Tokyo Olympics as one of the favourites in the 400m. In her preparations she had run 800m a handful of times, using it to build stamina. She also qualified for the 800m behind two of her teammates.

She won silver in the 400m, being beaten by the Australian Betty Cuthbert. Bitterly disappointed (even though she had set a new European record), she almost went shopping instead of competing in the 800m; after all, she was only Britain's third hope in that event and her times hadn't been that impressive.

Her fiancé (GB Men's team captain, Robbie Brightwell) and her coach suggested that her problem in the 400m was expending too much energy in the races before the final. It seems that this advice may have hit home when she was finally persuaded to run the 800m.

She came fifth in her 800m heat. Then, having got through to the final, she found herself ranked as the slowest runner in the line-up. When the bell rang for the final lap, she was in sixth place. She started sprinting and closed a five-metre gap and won gold, setting a new world record in the process.

She said, 'I was quite ignorant of women's 800 metre running. Middle-distance running for women was still in its infancy and the 800m had only been run in Rome four years earlier for the first time. I knew nothing about it but being so naive was probably to my advantage. Ignorance was bliss.'[18]

She retired immediately after the Olympics and married Robbie. They have three sons – two professional footballers and another 400m runner. In 1965 she was appointed MBE and in 2009 inducted into the England Athletics Hall of Fame.

Jacqueline Bisset

Actress Jacqueline Bisset was raised in Tilehurst, where she lived for part of each year until recently. She was taught French by her mother, Arlene, who was an evacuee from France during World War II. Jacqueline's parents divorced and Jacqueline cared for her mother, who was diagnosed with multiple sclerosis when Jacqueline was 15. As a child Jacqueline took ballet classes. Later she took acting classes, partially funded by modelling jobs.

She has featured in many films since the late 1960s, including *Murder on the Orient Express* (1974), *Casino Royale* (the 1967 spoof version) and many French films. Starring in *The Deep*, she is credited with popularising 'wet T-shirt' competitions because of shots of her swimming underwater. The (male) director is quoted as having said, 'That T-shirt made me a rich man',[19] but Jacqueline is reported to have felt exploited and tricked by the way it was filmed and shamelessly used to promote the film.

In 2010 she was awarded the French Légion d'Honneur at the same ceremony as Olivia de Havilland, daughter of **Lilian Fontaine**.

In 2013 she won a Golden Globe award for the BBC TV series *Dancing on the Edge*.

Her film career has spanned more than 50 years.

Lisa Daniely

Lisa was born in Reading in 1929 as Mary Elizabeth A. Bodington, to a French mother. She studied at RADA 1947–48, then spent six months at Sarah Bernhardt Theatre, Paris. Debuting aged 21, she was a successful film and TV actress, playing lead in *Lilli Marlene* (1950), a British war film, in which she also sang 'Lili Marlene'. She played Queen Elizabeth II in the 1996 film *Princess in Love*. She has also appeared in many TV programmes, including *Dr Who* and *The Saint*. Lisa, who has credits for playing over 90 characters, later undertook voice-over work and died aged 84.

Cherith Mellor

Cherith, Reading born, is a stage, TV and film actress. Cherith left LAMDA in 1968, winning the Rodney Millington Award. After two years at the Nottingham Playhouse she appeared in four West End plays, and in regional theatres. In 1997 she appeared in the film *Mrs Brown*. On TV, she played long-running characters in *Sam* (1973), *The Voyage of Charles Darwin* (1978), *A Kind of Loving* (1982), *Drummonds* (1985), *Westbeach* (1993), and *Down to Earth* (2000). She also appeared in *Coronation Street*, *Within These Walls*, *Angels*, *A Fine Romance*, *Inspector Morse*, *Cracker*, *Casualty*, *The Bill*, *Doctors* and *Heartbeat* to name but a few.

Marianne Faithfull

Singer/songwriter and actress Marianne Faithfull was born in Hampstead. Her family moved to Reading, where she attended St Joseph's Convent School and performed at the Progress Theatre. Her parents divorced, her father going to live in a commune in Oxfordshire.

In 1964 she was spotted at a Rolling Stones party by their manager, Andrew Loog Oldham. She went on to have a hit with the song *As Tears Go By* written by Keith Richards and Mick Jagger, aged only 19. After a brief marriage to an artist, during which she had a son, Nicholas, she had a four-year relationship with Jagger.

In a parallel career she acted on stage and in film, including the 1968 film *Girl on a Motorcycle.*

A star in her teens, by the end of the 1960s she was addicted to drugs and alcohol, and lost custody of Nicholas. However, she made a comeback later in the 1970s.

More recently, participating in the TV programme *Who do you think you are?* meant investigating her family history, and this helped her better understand her mother, Eva, with whom she has had a difficult relationship. Eva, the daughter of an Austrian knight, had been raped by the Red Army during the liberation of Vienna in 1944 before coming to England.

Marianne has had many setbacks in her life, including breast cancer, hepatitis C, miscarriage and living on the street as a heroin addict.

She has come through this with remarkable resilience. In recent years she has released more albums and even played God in the *Absolutely Fabulous* TV series. She has written a two-volume autobiography that documents a life almost synonymous with the 'Swinging Sixties' and a singing career spanning more than 50 years and 20 albums.

Sally Oldfield

Born in Dublin, singer songwriter Sally Oldfield grew up in Reading. She attended St Joseph's Convent School, the same school as **Marianne Faithfull**, with whom she was to become friends. She received a scholarship to the Royal Academy of Dancing. In 1968 she formed a duo, Sallyangie, with her younger brother Mike.

She performed in various bands and provided background vocals on several of Mike's albums including *Tubular Bells*. In 1978 her first solo album *Water Bearer* included her UK hit, 'Mirrors'. She has since released a number of solo and collaborative albums and is very popular in the Netherlands and Germany.

Iris Pridham

At the Pride of Reading Awards in 2017 Iris was the highly deserving winner of the Community Champion award, for her amazing dedication as a foster mother. Over a 36-year period Iris has fostered 67 children and babies in addition to raising her own three daughters. The duration of the fostering periods ranged from a few days to over 11 years. She also managed nine years of additional child minding.

Her daughter Marie said, 'The school run was like the Pied Piper, with not only foster children but also the children my mum child-minded.'[20]

Iris, who loved to take the children for picnics in Reading's Forbury Gardens, said, 'It can be challenging but you get so much out of it, which outweighs the challenges.'[21]

Ivy Hewitt

Ivy came over from Jamaica in the early 1950s. She was active in many community organisations, including Reading Council for Racial Equality, Age Concern, Reading Central Youth, Community Provision and Apollo Youth Club. Perhaps most importantly she was a founding member of Reading's West Indian Women's Circle. Peter Small, a trustee, paid tribute to her after her death: 'Ivy was one of the most caring and affectionate people I have ever met or worked with'.[22]

Ivy was a State Enrolled Nurse and worked at Reading's Battle and Royal Berkshire Hospitals and Townlands Hospital in Henley. After a break to raise a family she returned to work as a health visitor.

In 2004 the Reading Refocus charity honoured her with a community contribution award as part of its Black History Month celebrations.

Sally Taylor

Reading-born Sally Taylor is an alumna of Reading's Abbey School. Initially she taught English in Leicester. Best known for presenting *South Today* on BBC television, she has also presented on BBC Radio Solent and written a weekly column for the *Southern Daily Echo*. She was appointed MBE for regional broadcasting in 2005. In 2007 she broadcast from the Royal Navy Ice Patrol vessel HMS Endurance in Antarctica. She is involved in a number of charities and received an honorary doctorate from Winchester University in 2015. She is a patron of HIV and AIDS charity the Ribbon Centre.

Sangeeta Bhabra

A school career adviser suggested journalism to Sangeeta, because she liked talking and was very good at English. She worked for *The Reading Chronicle* newspaper and County Sound Radio before landing a job as a co-presenter of ITV News Meridian (which covers the greater Reading area several times a day).

Babita Sharma

Babita's parents came from India in the 1960s and opened a corner shop in Reading, where Babita grew up. Babita has written a book, *The Corner Shop,* which relates her experience of living at the shop in the context of British history of the last 50 years, and it has been a BBC Radio 4 'Book of the Week'. Babita studied Journalism, Film and Broadcasting at Cardiff University. This was followed by jobs with BBC Radio Wales, Thames Valley TV, BBC Radio Berkshire, *South Today* and a stint doing television and radio in Dubai. Babita, currently a BBC news anchor, has been named as one of the BBC's 'Talents to Watch' and is a BAME (Black, Asian and Minority Ethnic) spokesperson and mentors other BAME journalists.

Laura Tobin

After reading Physics and Meteorology at the University of Reading, Laura worked for the Meteorological Office. There she worked at various Royal Air Force bases providing forecasts for pilots, and then became a BBC weather reporter.

She has appeared on a number of celebrity game shows, including *Pointless Celebrities*.

In 2017 she succeeded in stuffing and folding 11 pancakes in 60 seconds, setting a new Guinness World Record. In 2015 she participated in the second **Edith Morley** Lecture at the University of Reading. She is the weather reporter on ITV's *Good Morning Britain*.

Lucy Benjamin

Born in Reading, Lucy attended the Redroofs Theatre School in Maidenhead. Aged 10, she played Sue in the stage musical *Wurzel Gummidge* alongside Jon Pertwee. She also appeared in *Dr Who* as a child. Initially she acted under her real name Lucy (Jane) Baker, but later changed her surname to Benjamin, the name of her brother. Lucy is best known for playing Lisa Fowler, a suspect in the 'Who shot Phil?' storyline in the BBC TV soap *EastEnders* (from 1998 to 2003) and in featured storylines on and off, ever since.

She has appeared in reality programmes including *I'm a Celebrity Get Me Out of Here* and ITV's *X Factor Battle of the Stars*, which she won.

A victim of the *Daily Mail* phone hacking scandal, she received a six-figure compensation payout after the Leveson enquiry.

She has appeared in numerous television shows, including *Press Gang, New Tricks, Kingdom, Holby City, Detectorists, Jupiter Moon* and *Casualty*. In 2013 she toured the UK in the *Hairspray* musical.

Fiona Talkington

Reading-born Fiona Talkington attended St Joseph's Convent School and the University of Reading.

A well-known radio presenter, she started her career with Reading's Radio 210 and has been with BBC Radio 3 for 30 years. She has presented on the BBC's Radio 4, World Service and 6 Music. Her extensive radio work includes *Late Junction*, the *BBC Proms* and live broadcasts from festivals such as WOMAD.

Fiona curates and directs music events for venues such as the Royal Opera House, the National Jazz Stage in Oslo and the Reading Fringe Festival.

She has been heavily involved in Norwegian arts for many years. This came about through befriending a Norwegian band on a trip to Missouri. In 2009 she was awarded the Royal Norwegian Order of Merit for services to the Norwegian arts scene.

She writes for *Songlines* magazine and sometimes for national papers and overseas publications.

In 2008 Fiona was diagnosed with breast cancer and treated at the Royal Berkshire Hospital. She is passionate about healthcare services, and has worked with cancer charities and on raising awareness of hidden disabilities and chronic pain issues.

Lucy Worsley

Born in Reading where she attended the Abbey School, as a child Lucy moved around quite a bit to exotic (but cold) places such as Iceland, because her father, an academic at the University of Reading, was a geologist specialising in glaciers and permafrost.

Lucy read Ancient and Modern History at Oxford, even though her father had said that if she did so she would 'end up cleaning toilets for a living'.[23] This has turned out not to be the case, although she is something of an expert on Henry VIII's toilet habits. Reputedly her most-used phrase concerns the king having a dedicated servant – 'The Groom of the Stool' – whose chief role involved a cloth that today would be replaced with toilet paper. There was an additional servant, 'the Necessary Woman', whose job was to empty the chamber pot. Lucy has said 'womankind has come a long way since then'.[24]

Lucy went on to do a doctorate at the University of Sussex. She has worked as an Inspector of Historic Buildings for English Heritage and as a curator at Milton Manor. At the time of writing she is chief curator of Historic Royal Palaces – an organisation that looks after the unoccupied royal palaces in London such as the Tower of London and Hampton Court.

Having to give talks and guided tours as a curator, television was a natural next step. Starting her TV career in 2011, she is a popular presenter of TV history programmes, which she often presents dressed up as historic characters.

Her television career hasn't been hindered by a slight speech impediment – to date she has presented over thirty TV programmes. These cover diverse subjects with titles such as *Tales from the Royal Bedchamber*, *Dancing Cheek To Cheek: An Intimate History Of Dance*, *Empire of the Tsars: Romanov Russia*, *British History's Biggest Fibs*, *American History's Biggest Fibs* and *Suffragettes*.

Lucy has also written a number of books, including a biography of **Jane Austen** and *Eliza Rose*, a children's novel. In 2018 she was appointed OBE for services to history and heritage for services to history and heritage.

Lucy is a keen runner and, in her teens, represented her county at cross-country.

Miranda Krestovnikoff

Miranda was born in Buckinghamshire and attended Reading's Abbey School. She read Zoology at Bristol University. She then found a job with the acclaimed BBC Natural History Unit, starting as a runner and progressing to researcher. She has become a television presenter covering a diverse range of subjects, although her passion is for wildlife. She is a very highly qualified and experienced diver, and this often features in her television appearances. At the time of writing she is president of the Royal Society for the Protection of Birds (RSPB), a role which she took over from **Kate Humble** in 2013. Miranda is also an accomplished musician and singer. She plays for the New Bristol Sinfonia and has formed her own a cappella group.

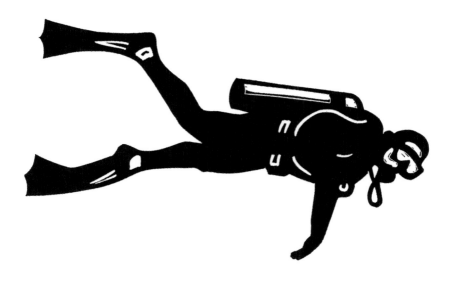

Molly Hide

Molly was born in 1913 in Shanghai, China, where her father ran a business. The family returned to England when she was four. Molly learnt to play cricket at school and went on to study for a Diploma in Agriculture at the University of Reading. Her family had a Surrey farm, which she worked on in parallel with a cricketing career.

Molly played in the first women's test match, between Australia and England, held in Brisbane in 1934. In 1937 she became England captain, a position that she held for 17 years. Although better known for her batting, she was also a successful spin bowler. Molly's test match (amateur) career spanned 20 years, although for 11 of those there were no tests due to the Second World War. Over 15 test matches Molly made 872 runs (36.33 average), and took 36 wickets (15.25 runs per wicket) and 10 catches.

After retiring from playing, Molly continued her involvement in cricket and in 1973 became president of the Women's Cricket Association. She was involved in selection, management and broadcasting. When the England Women's team won the 1993 World Cup at Lords, Molly was a guest of honour.

Once described as 'the personification of women's cricket'[25], Molly also played lacrosse for the national team. She died aged 81.

Claire Taylor

Claire's cricketing prowess was apparent early on, when she captained her school team to success in the Wigley's Cricket County Championship. She attended the Dolphin School in Hurst, and Abbey and Kendrick Schools in Reading. Her first international sporting success wasn't in cricket, but hockey; she was an international in the under 17 and under 19 age groups.

Claire read Mathematics at Oxford, where she won three blues for hockey and three half-blues for cricket. After graduation she worked in IT before deciding to be a professional cricketer. In 1998 a One Day International (ODI) against Australia marked the start of a 13-year international cricketing career with over 150 international appearances for England.

Claire has been described as 'the best batter in the women's game',[26] but her mental toughness is also legendary. A former coach,

Mark Lane, has been quoted as saying, 'It's her ability to think several overs ahead and work the field around which makes her the world No. 1'.[27] Claire played for Reading, Thames Valley and Berkshire Women's cricket clubs for many years.

In 2009 the English women's team won both the women's cricket World Cup (ODI format) and the T20 World Cup, and in both Claire was declared player of the tournament, indicating how vital her performance was to England's success. Richly deserved accolades followed. Claire became the first woman to become Wisden's Cricketer of the Year. Both the International Cricket Council (ICC) and the England and Wales Cricket Board (ECB) declared her their woman cricketer of the year. Since retirement in 2011 she has obtained an MA in Applied Management from the Henley Business School and worked as a management consultant based at the University of Reading. Claire was appointed MBE in 2010 and inducted into the ICC Hall of Fame in 2018.

Molly Hide and Claire Taylor showing changes to batting apparel over several decades

Kate Winslet

Kate Winslet was born and raised in Reading into a theatrical family – her parents were both stage actors and her grandparents founded the Reading Rep theatre. She attended the Redroofs Theatre School in Maidenhead. In her first job, at age 11, she acted alongside the Honey Monster in a Sugar Puffs breakfast cereal advertisement.

Following her film debut in *Heavenly Creatures* (1994), she triumphed over 100 other hopefuls in an audition for an adaptation of **Jane Austen**'s *Sense and Sensibility* (1995), leading to the first of several Oscar nominations. Her big breakthrough was starring in *Titanic* (1997) alongside Leonardo Di Caprio, at the time the most expensive film ever made. She won the Best Actress Oscar in 2009 for *The Reader*. She has acted in many films since, receiving her seventh Academy Award nomination for the film *Steve Jobs* (2015), in which she portrayed Joanna Hoffman, Jobs' marketing chief.

Kate is active in promoting autism awareness. She is a co-founder of The Golden Hat Foundation that works in the field and has published a book that was featured in the UN's World Autism Day in 2012.

She has spoken publicly about how she was teased and bullied at school, called 'blubber' and told that she would have to settle for 'fat girl parts'[28]; how wrong they were!

In the 2012 Queen's Birthday Honours she was awarded Commander of the Order of the British Empire (CBE) for her services to drama.

Anna Winslet

Anna Winslet is **Kate Winslet**'s older actress sister. She has appeared in the films *Empty Mirror* (2000), *Red Rose* (2004), and *Somnolence* (2009). Anna also acted in *The Cater Street Hangman* (1998), based on an Anne Perry novel. An interesting connection is that Anne Perry was born Juliet Hulme, changing her name following her involvement in a murder. **Kate Winslet** portrayed Juliet Hulme in the film about that murder, *Heavenly Creatures* (1994).

Beth Winslet

Beth Winslet, **Kate Winslet's** younger sister, made her acting debut aged 19 in television production *The Scold's Bridle*. She has appeared in several films, including *Bodywork* (2001), *Exitz* (2007), *The Hybrid* (2014) and *The Real Jane Austen* (2002).

Kate Richardson-Walsh

Kate Walsh played hockey for Reading for seven years and captained the England team for 13 of her 17 years as an international player. With over 370 caps, she is the most capped female player in Great Britain.

As captain she led England to win the European Championships in 2015, and played in the squads that collected two bronzes and two silvers in the Commonwealth Games between 2002 and 2014. Her achievements as GB captain in the Olympic Games are memorable.

In GB's first match in the London 2012 Olympics Kate was hit in the face by a Japanese player's hockey stick during a tackle. She had to have surgery for a broken jaw. Amazingly, with a plate in her jaw and wearing a face mask, she returned to play in later matches during the competition, leading the team to a bronze medal.

In 2013 Kate married fellow GB team player **Helen Richardson**. They both adopted Richardson-Walsh as their surname.

In the 2016 Olympics in Rio, Kate captained the GB team, which included Helen. They became the first same-sex married couple playing in the same team to win an Olympic medal. Triumphantly, that medal was gold. In 2016, Richardson-Walsh was the first hockey player to be shortlisted for BBC Sports Personality of the Year and in 2017 she was appointed OBE.

Helen Richardson-Walsh

Helen, the wife of **Kate Richardson-Walsh**, is also a former Reading Hockey Club player who was in the GB Olympic bronze- and gold-winning teams. She has amassed over 290 international caps for England and GB and and was appointed MBE at the same time her wife Kate was appointed OBE.

Alex Danson

Alex made her international hockey debut at 16. She has played for Reading Hockey Club. A forward, she is joint record goal-scorer for England and Great Britain, having scored 115 goals in 306 appearances. She was joint top goal scorer at the 2016 Rio Olympics when the GB team won gold, and had also helped the team to win bronze at the London 2012 Olympics. In 2017 she became captain of the England and GB teams.

A freak accident in 2018 whilst on holiday in Kenya left her with a mild traumatic brain injury and after failing to get back to playing 18 months later, she retired from the game.

Alex has started a hockey academy to introduce children to the game. In 2017 she was appointed MBE.

Deborah Flood

Debbie was born in Yorkshire, coming to Reading to read Physiology and Biochemistry at the University. As a youngster she was very sporty, participating in cross-country running, 1500m and shot put. She represented GB in judo before taking up rowing. In the 1998 Junior World Rowing Championships she won a bronze in double sculls, followed by a gold in the under 23 World Championships a year later. In 2000 she won gold in single sculls at the world championships.

Whilst studying at Reading she competed in the Athens 2004 Olympics, winning a silver medal in quadruple sculls. She again won silver in the 2008 Beijing Olympic Games. Debbie has three World Championship titles for the quadruple sculls and one for single sculls. In 2013 Debbie became the first female captain of the Leander Club in Henley, one of the most famous rowing clubs in the world and over 200 years old.

Debbie is a committed Christian and has worked helping prisoners and disruptive young people.

Artist's impression of Debbie and Anna if they were to row together in the same boat.

Anna Watkins

Anna spent her childhood in Staffordshire. She went on to study Natural Sciences at Cambridge and then gain a PhD in Mathematics from the University of Reading. At Cambridge she started rowing and was picked for a national talent programme. Her first international rowing outing was at the 2004 Under 23 World Championships, where her coxless four won gold. She won a bronze in the double sculls at the Beijing Olympics in 2008. In the London 2012 Olympics she and partner Katherine Grainger won gold at Eton Dorney, beating Australia in the final and setting a new Olympic record. As well as Olympic honours, Anna has two world titles and was appointed an MBE in 2013 for services to rowing. Having retired from competitive rowing, Anna consults on sports data analytics and is a patron of the Women's Sport Trust, which promotes women's sport and welfare.

Rebecca Cooke

Reading girl Rebecca started her competitive swimming career as a member of Reading Swimming Club. She competed in the 2000 Sydney and 2004 Athens Olympics, preparing for Sydney and her A-levels at the same time. At both Sydney and Athens she made it through to the 800m freestyle final.

Rebecca moved to Glasgow after finishing her A-levels in 2001 to remain with her Australian coach Stephen Hill, who had taken a position there. She is partially deaf due to a virus caught as a toddler, so doesn't hear the two-lap whistle in the 800m. Also very short-sighted, she struggles to read the finishing order on the board and has been known to ask a competitor in an adjacent lane whether she won or came second in a race.

Rebecca won gold in the 400m and 800m freestyle at the 2002 Manchester Commonwealth Games, retaining the 800m title four years later at Melbourne where she also won a silver for the 400m individual medley. She has won bronze medals at World Championship level, silver in European Championships and has broken British records on six occasions.

Rebecca retired from elite swimming at 24, having failed to make selection for the 2008 Beijing Olympics. She has been awarded life membership of Reading Swimming Club.

Natalie Dormer

Natalie is half Welsh and part Norwegian. She was born in Reading and attended the Chiltern Edge and Blue Coat Schools. She was bullied at school, but never knew why. She had a conditional offer for Cambridge University, but failing to get the necessary 'A' in her history A-level she went to drama school instead.

Her film debut was in *Casanova* (2005). Playing the part of Victoria, her comic timing was so good that the director had her part expanded.

Natalie had half her head shaved in order to play Cressida in *The Hunger Games: Mockingjay – Parts* 1 and 2. Other appearances include the film *Captain America: The First Avenger* (2011), the BBC TV court drama *Silk*, playing Anne Boleyn in the television series *The Tudors* and starring in *Picnic at Hanging Rock* (2018).

She is probably best known for playing Margaery Tyrell in *Game of Thrones*. She has also starred in *In Darkness,* which she co-wrote, in which she plays a blind musician who witnesses a murder.

Natalie has run the London Marathon for charity, finishing in an impressive sub four hours.

Jessica Swale

Jessica was brought up in Reading in a house full of books. With that, an English teacher mother, and a love of dressing up, it is no surprise that Jessica Swale fell in love with theatre.

As a pupil at Kendrick School, which had no drama department at the time, Jessica asked the Head if they could have a school play. The answer was yes – as long as she organised it. Jessica recalls, 'Five years later, eight school plays under my belt, I was off to Exeter University to study directing with a new spring in my step and a passion to train properly – and work with actors that weren't exclusively teenage and female. I didn't realise then how unusual it was for a woman to want to be a director.'[29]

After Exeter she studied directing at the Central School of Speech and Drama and became Associate director for the Out of Joint Theatre Company at the National Theatre. During this time, she set up and ran Red Handed Theatre Company, with whom she has been nominated for and won several awards.

Jessica Swale © Michael Wharley

In 2012 Jessica tried her hand at writing a play. *Blue Stockings* 'follows the trials and tribulations of the young pioneering women who were the first female university students in the UK – and the backlash they faced'.[30] It was premiered at Shakespeare's Globe theatre, was a hit, and became part of the GCSE syllabus.

Her next play, *Nell Gwynn,* won an Olivier award and transferred to the West End. It is due to be released as a feature film with a screenplay written by Jessica.

Other plays include a choral work, *Thomas Tallis*, and adaptations of *The Jungle Book, Sense and Sensibility, Far from the Madding Crowd* and *Stig of the Dump.*

More recently she has become involved in film. Screenwriting credits include *Horrible Histories – The Movie!* and shortly to be released adaptations of *Longbourn* and **Jane Austen**'s *Persuasion.* Her first feature as writer-director, *Summerland,* stars Gemma Arterton and Tom Courtenay. Jessica says, 'I moved into film because it gives me a chance to combine my two passions, writing and directing. There is nothing quite like making a piece of work from scratch and seeing it through every moment of its gestation, from those thrilling first seeds, through the writing graft, the making, casting, directing, editing and out the other side. I find that so creatively satisfying and film, happily, accords me that opportunity.'[31]

Jessica, a passionate advocate of diversity in drama, is an active spokeswoman with the Time's Up movement. Her short comic film *Leading Lady Parts* about discrimination in the film industry has had 25 million YouTube views. She has worked with Youth Bridge Global, an international NGO, making theatre in war-torn and developing countries including Kosovo and the Marshall Islands.

Fran Kirby

Fran joined her home club, Reading Football Club, at the age of 7 and turned out to be something of a footballing prodigy. At the age of 16 she was playing for the first team.

At 14 Fran lost her mother suddenly to a brain haemorrhage. This led to depression and giving up football at 17. Two years later she was back playing for Reading, scoring 33 goals in her first season. She became the first at Reading FC Women to turn professional. In the 2014 season Reading came third in the Women's Super League (WSL) second league, helped along by Fran, who was the top scorer in the two top divisions with 29 goals in 22 games.

In 2015 Fran was included in the squad for the FIFA Women's World Cup in Canada, where England finished third. That year she trans-ferred to Chelsea FC, playing a major part in Chelsea winning the WSL. Chelsea also won the Women's FA Cup, but Fran was unable to play for them in the cup as she had played for Reading in earlier rounds.

During the 2016/17 season Fran was dogged by injury, which prevented her from participating in Chelsea's FA Cup campaign.

Chelsea again attained the double in the 2017/18 season, Fran's influence being felt in both competitions, and she scored a goal in the FA Cup final. She was voted the PFA Player's Player of the Year and the Football Writers Women's Footballer of the Year.

In 2019 she was a member of the World Cup squad and scored in the third-place playoff against Sweden.

Fara Williams

At the age of 17 Fara started playing for the Chelsea first team, making her debut as a senior player. During her career she has played for Liverpool; Everton, which she captained; and Arsenal, winning the Women's FA Cup with the latter two. In 2017 she joined Reading FC Women.

The midfielder has played in three World Cups, four European (Euro) Cups, and the 2012 Olympics. With over 165 caps, she is England's most capped player. She captained the England team that reached the Euro 2009 final, losing to Germany. Phil Neville said 'she stands alone as one of the greatest footballers England has ever produced on both the men's and the women's side'.[32]

During her early career and following a family breakdown she was homeless for about six years, moving from hostel to hostel while she was playing for England. She has since worked with homeless charities, especially Homeless FA. In 2016 she was appointed MBE for services to women's football and charity.

Coralie Bickford-Smith

Coralie studied Typography and Graphic Communication at the University of Reading. Working in-house at Penguin Books, she has designed a highly acclaimed series of covers for the clothbound Penguin Classics, including a complete set of **Jane Austen** novels.

Coralie has written and illustrated her own books. The first, *The Fox and The Star*, is beautifully illustrated, with the design influenced by William Blake and William Morris. The story, written for children but also to appeal to adults, has a theme of loss – it is about a fox who loses his only friend, the star. The book beat stiff competition to win the Waterstones Book of the Year award in 2015 and has been listed in *Time Out's* 100 Best Children's Books of All Time.

She published her second book, *The Worm and the Bird*, in 2017.

Coralie was awarded an Honorary Doctorate in Literature by the University of Reading in 2017.

Suzanne Stallard

Suzanne, born in Reading and raised on the Dee Road Estate, is known as the inspirational founder and director of local charity Jelly. Jelly has been energetically promoting creative arts in Reading for many years. Its biggest annual event is the *Open for Art* festival that sees art and creativity peppered across the town. Jelly also provides studio space for artists, works with schools and runs workshops.

Fortunately for Reading, Suzanne decided to pursue a career in art, despite being told at school that that was the last thing she should do. She studied for a degree in Fine Art in Bristol. She founded Jelly in 1993; it was originally called *Jelly Leg'd Chicken* – the name chosen so that it didn't sound like a gallery. She says, 'I knew I liked to work with other people... there was nowhere to go if you wanted to experience art'.[33]

In addition to encouraging and supporting the artistic endeavours of others, Suzanne herself paints and draws and pursues activism through art.

Suzanne is involved in many other organisations in Reading, including the homeless charity Launchpad as chair of the trustees, and is on the board of Reading Rep theatre.

Suzanne Stallard © Salvo Toscano

Mary Genis

Mary Genis's parents came to Britain from Trinidad and Tobago during the Windrush era and Mary was born in London. She started out in costume design and as a freelance musician but over the years her varied roles have included singer, instrumental musician, producer, visual artist, performance artist, publisher and costume designer. In 1997 she set up the Reading All Steel Percussion Orchestra (RASPO), a community steel band which has performed in the Notting Hill Carnival, at WOMAD, the Royal Festival Hall and the 2012 Olympics where Mary also participated as a dancer in the Paralympics opening ceremony.

Mary founded Culture Mix as an umbrella for her many initiatives. Through the organisation she encourages participation in the arts by young people. Culture Mix provides steel pan education to schools and supports youngsters embarking on a career in the creative arts through vocational training and job opportunities. It produces events showcasing African and Caribbean culture.

Mary is a trustee of the Reading arts organisation Jelly; Reading Refocus, which mentors young people, and the Carnival Village Trust which organises the Notting Hill Carnival. Her influence in Reading has clearly contributed to the cultural richness of the town.

~~Taylor Swift~~ Hannah (Callowhill) Penn

Singer-songwriter Taylor Swift, born in Reading, Berks, *Pennsylvania*, to Terry's dismay doesn't qualify for inclusion in this book (sorry Terry). In 2019 Taylor was listed by Forbes as one of the 100 most powerful women in the world. However, having strayed to Pennsylvania, we stumbled across another woman who qualifies for inclusion. Had Forbes existed then, they might well have listed her as one of the most powerful women of the 18th century.

Hannah Callowhill, born 1671, became the second wife of William Penn, the founder and proprietor of Pennsylvania, at the time a privately held colony. In 1709 the Penn family moved to Ruscombe, near Reading (the one in England).

In 1712 William suffered strokes, becoming incapacitated. Hannah took over the proprietorship of Pennsylvania, governing in his place for six years. Although she had a deputy governor on site she was actively involved, negotiating disputes with Maryland over the joint border, and with the British government over issues with Pennsylvanian law.

The Penns were Quakers who promoted freedom of religion, representative government and public education, amongst other things. They were frequent visitors to The Quaker meeting house in Reading's London Street, where Reading International Solidarity Centre (RISC) is now located. There have been reports that William still occasionally visits in ghostly form.

In 1984 President Reagan of the United States proclaimed Hannah and William Penn honorary citizens of the United States of America, stating Hannah 'devoted her life to the pursuit of peace and justice'.[34]

Notes

1   *The Association Game: A History of British Football*, Matthew Taylor, Pearson Education, 2008
2   *Oxford Dictionary of National Biography*, OUP, 2004
3   Entrepreneur Tutu is an 'inspiration to young black women and girls', inyourarea.co.uk, 11 June 2018
4   *Jane Austen: A Family Record*, Deirdre Le Faye, William Austen-Leigh, Richard Arthur Austen-Leigh, p. 50. British Library, 1989.
5   *Jane Austen: A Family Record,* p. 81
6   Extraordinary women of The MERL and University of Reading Special Collections (merl.reading.ac.uk/wp-content/uploads/sites/20/2018/08/3238-B21448-Extraordinary-women-MM-v11-WEB-FINAL.pdf)
7   *A Bigness of Heart: Phoebe Cusden of Reading*, Adam Stout. Reading–Düsseldorf Association, 1997.
8   *A Bigness of Heart.*
9   *A Bigness of Heart.*
10   'Kate Humble urges everyone to enjoy nature by getting naked', Claire Carter, *Daily Telegraph,* 7 September 2014
11   Elizabeth Taylor, johnsonandalcock.co.uk, accessed 8 December 2019
12   'At Mrs. Taylor's', Kingsley Amis, *The Spectator,* 14 June 1957
13   'How the Other Elizabeth Taylor Reconciled Family Life and Art', Namara Smith, *The New Yorker,* 16 June 2015
14   *Angel*, Virago, 6 April 2006
15   *Oxford Dictionary of National Biography*
16   *Oxford Dictionary of National Biography*

17 *Oxford Dictionary of National Biography*

18 Rider's legends: Ann Packer, bbc.co.uk, 26 September 2000

19 '14 unnecessarily revealing movie costumes', *Daily Telegraph,*
    14 November 2017

20 Foster mum wins Pride of Reading Award after 30 years of caring for
    children', *getreading*, 5 November 2017

21 Foster mum wins Pride of Reading Award after 30 years of caring for
    children', *getreading*, 5 November 2017

22 'Ivy Hewitt was true champion', *getreading,* 7 Jun 2013

23 'Lucy Worsley interview: "My father said I would end up cleaning toilets"',
    Julia Llewellyn Smith, *The Times*, 14 December 2019

24 'Sixty Seconds with Lucy Worsley', Amanda Cable, metro.news,
    12 May 2019

25 OBITUARY: Molly Hide, *The Independent*, 13 September 1995

26 'England star Claire Taylor quits international cricket', bbc.com, 8 July 2011

27 'Claire Taylor, Wisden's First Lady', Scyld Berry, Wisden.com,
    25 September 2019

28 'Kate Winslet gives biggest f*** you to bullies', metro.co.uk, 23 March 2017

29 private communication

30 private communication

31 private communication

32 'Fara Williams: Phil Neville says midfielder's England career is not over',
    bbb.com, 8 May 2019

33 'The Jelly Family', jelly.org.uk, accessed 29 February 2020

34 *United States Statutes at Large*, Volume 99, Part 2, Proclamation 5284

Further reading

Oxford Dictionary of National Biography, OUP, 2004

A Bigness of Heart: Phoebe Cusden of Reading, Adam Stout, Reading–Düsseldorf Association, 1997

Lettice Curtis: Her Autobiography, Lettice Curtis, Red Kite, 2004

The Celebrated Reading Sauce: Charles Cocks & Co. Ltd. 1789–1962, TAB Corley, Berkshire Archeological Journal vol 70

Jane Austen: A family record, Deirdre Le Faye, Cambridge University Press, 2004

Before and After: Edith Morley, edited by Barbara Morris, Two Rivers Press, 2016

Women Workers in Seven Professions, Edith Morley, George Routledge & Sons Ltd, 1914

Images of England Miles Aircraft, Rod Simpson, NPI Media Group, 1998

Skirting the Boundary: A History of Women's Cricket, Isabelle Duncan, The Robson Press, 2013

Evelyn Dunbar: A life in Painting, Christopher Campbell-Howes, Romarin, 2016

Alma Cogan: A Memoir, Sandra Caron, Bloomsbury Publishing PLC, 1991

Reading: The Place of the Red One, Duncan Mackay, Two Rivers Press, 2016

Local websites & archives

Museum of English Rural Life (MERL)
merl.reading.ac.uk

University of Reading
www.reading.ac.uk

Reading Museum
www.readingmuseum.org.uk

Thames Valley Police museum
www.thamesvalley.police.uk/police-forces/thames-valley-police/areas/
au/about-us/who-we-are/thames-valley-police-museum/

Reading Central Library
www.reading.gov.uk/libraries

Jane Austen House Museum
www.janeaustens.house

Reading Football Club
www.readingfc.co.uk

David Nash Ford's Royal County of Berkshire History Website
www.berkshirehistory.com

Museum of Berkshire Aviation
www.museumofberkshireaviation.co.uk

ATA exhibition at Maidenhead heritage centre
www.maidenheadheritage.org.uk

Two Rivers Press has been publishing in and about Reading
since 1994. Founded by the artist Peter Hay (1951–2003), the press
continues to delight readers, local and further afield, with its varied list
of individually designed, thought-provoking books.